Ten Key Events in Jesus' Life

Bible Basics for Adults

by John R. Bucka

Leader Guide

Augsburg Fortress, Minneapolis

Contents

OVERVIEW 3

USING THE LEADER GUIDE 3

ABOUT THE LEARNER 5

COURSE INTRODUCTION 7

1 A NEW BEGINNING 8
The Birth of Jesus (Luke 2:1-20)
The Baptism of Jesus (Matthew 3:13-17)

2 BEYOND THE LIMITS 10
The Temptation of Jesus (Luke 4:1-13)
The Cleansing of the Temple (Mark 11:15-19)

3 OUTSIDE THE CIRCLE 12
The Sermon on the Mount (Matthew 5:1-12)
The Healing of the Paralytic (Mark 2:1-12)

4 GIVEN AND SHED FOR YOU 14
The Lord's Supper (Matthew 26:17-30)
The Crucifixion (Mark 15:21-39)

5 AFTER WE SAY GOOD-BYE 16
The Road to Emmaus (Luke 24:13-35)
The Ascension (Acts 1:6-11)

6 MORE THAN JUST DETAILS 18
Review and Summary (John 14:6)

DISCUSSION STRATEGIES 20

REPRODUCIBLE PAGES 22

GLOSSARY 32

BIBLE BASICS FOR ADULTS
Ten Key Events in Jesus' Life Leader Guide
This leader guide has a corresponding learner book.

Editors: Mark Gardner and Eric P. Vollen
Designer: Craig P. Claeys
Illustrators: Judy Swanson and Parrot Graphics/Patti Isaacs

Unless otherwise noted, scripture quotations are from New Revised Standard Version Bible, copyright 1989 Division of Christian Education of the National Council of the Churches of Christ in the United States of America. Used by permission.

Copyright © 1996 Augsburg Fortress
All rights reserved. May not be reproduced with the exception of the materials on pages 22-30.

ISBN 0-8066-2328-4

Manufactured in U.S.A.

1 2 3 4 5 6 7 8 9 0 1 2 3 4 5 6 7 8 9

Overview

FEWER AND FEWER ADULTS feel comfortable studying the Bible alone or with others. **Bible Basics for Adults** resources address the needs of adults who may not know basic Bible stories or the importance of the Bible for daily Christian living. These four courses will make it easy for adults who know little about the Bible to study it.

General Objectives

The objectives of these courses are to help learners who are not familiar with the Bible and its stories to:
- gain familiarity with the Bible;
- see the Bible as important to their lives;
- gain confidence in using the Bible for their growth in faith and life;
- see their life stories—their joys, sorrows, relationships, and search for meaning—as part of the larger narrative of the people of God that is presented in the Bible.

Course Descriptions

The four courses and their descriptions are as follows:

1. Ten Key Events in Jesus' Life. This course helps adult learners gain a basic understanding of the life and ministry of Jesus. The central story of God's love is presented through the life, death, and resurrection of God's Son. The six sessions help adult learners connect their life stories with the biblical story of the identity and ministry of Jesus, to see in the life of Jesus and his disciples a connection between the Bible and the concerns and hopes of the contemporary world.

2. Ten Key People from the Bible. Adults are introduced to stories of important biblical characters. In this course, adult learners not only enjoy the study of the Bible through stories, but see in those accounts questions and issues that connect with their own lives and journey of faith today.

3. Ten Key Events from the Bible. While this study identifies the life, death, and resurrection of Jesus as the pivotal event of history and the source of our meaning and hope, God's surprising and compassionate deeds help the learner to see that God's creative power has been at work throughout history and is at work in our journey of faith today.

4. Ten Key Passages from the Bible. This course presents biblical themes that are central to the Christian faith. Through this study participants will celebrate the Christian message in both the Old and New Testament. Living in a world often fraught with fears and disappointments, adults will be encouraged with the life of faith that is filled with prayer, praise, and thanksgiving.

Using the Leader Guide

LEADERS of the **Bible Basics for Adults** courses will discover a helpful new approach awaiting them as they explore each leader guide. Leaders will teach from a two-page session plan designed to allow easy access to ideas for each segment of class time.

Introductions. Each leader guide begins with these introductory resources:
- a description of the adult learner;
- help for using the leader guide to integrate the learners' life experiences in basic Bible study;
- a course introduction.

Session plans. Each two-page session plan begins with a theme statement that highlights a basic biblical concept shared by the session's two biblical texts.

The first five session plans follow this format:
- **Gathering.** An idea for community building and introducing the session theme;
- **Read the Story.** A strategy for reading the first Bible text of the session;
- **Expand the Story.** Ways to discover what the text says about God, the people of God, and the learners;
- **Read the Story.** A strategy for reading the second Bible text of the session;
- **Expand the Story.** Ways to discover what the text says about God, the people of God, and the learners;
- **Focus the Stories.** Activities that focus on the connections learners are able to make between their lives and the two featured Bible texts.

The sixth session plan follows a similar format but focuses on one biblical text. Leaders will choose activities from each part of the session that best meet the needs of the learners. To prepare for an activity listed on a session plan, a leader may be directed to another page in the guide for the following helps:

Discussion strategies. Ways to involve all learners in actively identifying, sharing, and scrutinizing their opinions and life experiences.

Reproducible pages. Ways to expand, not replace, the activities in the learner book. These include process helps that the learner book cannot accomodate. They are referred to in specific session plans and need to be reproduced before the session for use during or after each session.

Common Resources

All four Bible Basics for Adults courses contain a number of pages that can be copied, distributed, and discussed throughout any of the courses. Or this material may be copied and distributed for the learners' reading enjoyment.

LEARNER BOOK

- **How the Bible Is Organized (page 23).** This reproducible page gives a simple outline of the books of the Bible. Copies of this outline may be distributed to learners at the beginning of the course to help them identify Old and New Testament books and to locate biblical texts more easily for reading and study.
- **Bible Time Line (pages 24-25).** The time line helps learners put the Bible texts they are studying in each course into the larger context of God's salvation story as documented by Scripture. As you begin the study of each text, refer the learners to the time line to help them appreciate the scope and sequence of God at work in the lives of God's people.
- **How to Read the Bible (page 26).** This page provides three tools for beginning Bible readers. "Finding a Bible Reference" shows learners how to interpret a reference and then track down the passage in the Bible. "Going Deeper" provides questions to help learners dig into and apply a text. Bible readers who want to keep notes in their Bibles about their discoveries and questions will find "Marking Your Bible" useful.

- **Glossary (inside back cover).** The glossary in each course defines key words and phrases in that course, and it is placed in the learner book so it is always available to learners. Note that glossary entries pertinent to each session are identified in a prominent place on each session plan in this guide. Make sure learners understand these words and phrases before the end of each session.

LEADER GUIDE

- **Bible Study Resources (page 26).** All of us have questions about what we read in the Bible. This reproducible page provides a brief description of the various types of references, including the study Bible, cross-reference, commentary, handbook, dictionary, and atlas. Particularly helpful is the explanation of how to use a concordance.
- **Bible Bookmarks (page 27).** Copy this reproducible page and cut out markers to help give learners quick access to the key texts being studied. They can also be used for reflection and prayer at various times between sessions. This serves as a way to connect biblical learning with one's daily life. During the first session, explore with the learners how these bookmarks can be used.
- **Old and New Testament Maps (pages 28-29).** These reproducible maps help learners find important biblical locations in relationship to the Middle East today. Old and New Testament sites are identified on page 29. Make copies of these maps for each learner and refer to the maps at appropriate times during the sessions.
- **The Bible in Worship (page 30).** The Bible is at the center of Christian worship. From the Bible comes much of the content and the general form of our worship. This reproducible page discusses liturgy as the pattern of Bible texts we hear, sing, and pray in worship.
- **Using These Resources in Other Settings (page 31).** Because of the diverse schedules and interests of adult learners, other ways to use this resource are explored. Consider using these other settings as ways to reach more people with this and other Bible studies.

About the Learner

THESE RESOURCES ARE DESIGNED for adults who have an interest in learning basic Bible stories and exploring the importance of the Bible in daily Christian living. Researchers suggest that three quarters of adults in the church do not participate in Bible study. Add to this the number of adults joining churches, and the potential audience for basic Bible study is tremendous. Providing the opportunity to help adult learners become familiar with Bible stories, and to gain confidence in their ability to read and understand Scripture, to grow in faith, and to address the issues they face in their lives is a priority for church education leaders.

Getting Started

Adults choose to participate in Bible study groups for a variety of reasons. Research indicates that the following are important factors to consider as you establish Bible study groups in your church.

Adults participate when they believe the experience will help them grow in a way that will benefit them, their families, and their communities. Adults are motivated to finds ways to "make life work" as they face the challenges of daily living. Issues that arise from relationships, family, aging, job transitions, money, and a variety of circumstances as defined by the learners need to be addressed in Bible study groups.

Adults participate when they are sure they will not be embarrassed by their lack of biblical knowledge or insight. Many Bible study resources and leaders assume a level of familiarity with the Bible and biblical scholarship that most adults find overwhelming and disconnected from the issues of daily life. Walter Wink, a professor of biblical interpretation, suggests that adults seek insight and not just information. It is the intersection of the biblical text with the experience of the learner that evokes insight. Because we are all experts when it comes to our own experience, no one should be made to feel inadequate when it comes to studying the Bible. (Walter Wink, *Transforming Bible Study: A Leader's Guide* 2nd ed. [Nashville, Tenn: Abingdon Press, 1989], 37-38).

Adults participate when they are comfortable with the other learners in the group. Adults know that they will benefit from the opportunity to see and hear what life looks like from the perspective of others. They know that learning comes from asking, sharing, doing, and imagining. But the idea of sharing personal information with strangers can be a barrier to participation. Learners who have not participated in Bible study as adults are more likely to accept an invitation to join a group of people they know or who have similar concerns (for example, parents with teenagers) than they are to sign up for a group in response to an announcement in a bulletin or newsletter.

Adults participate when the time commitment honors their priorities. Finding a time to meet can be a difficult hurdle to overcome. Parents with young children may appreciate a group that meets every other Monday night rather than weekly. This allows them to be with their children and helps with finding child care. A group of older adults may prefer to meet during the day so they do not have to travel at night.

Recruiting

Keep the following suggestions in mind as you establish groups for basic Bible study:

Keep the groups small. This study focuses on the intersection between basic Bible texts and the learner's life experience. A group of 6 to 10 participants allows for a balance of individual reflection and group discussion that is important in this study.

Start with the groups that already exist in your church (parents with young children, new members, empty nesters, Sunday school teachers, young adults, and so on). People who share concerns and situations in life will be more comfortable together and may have similar schedules.

Make personal invitations. Announcements during worship, in bulletins or newsletters, and community papers are important. But many more adults will respond to a personal invitation to participate in a Bible study group. Make sure they know the details of the study, who else will be there, and the expectations of the participants.

Consider allowing the group to decide on the time and meeting place for the study.

Communicate clearly that this is a study for adults who are interested in learning basic Bible stories and exploring the importance of the Bible in daily Christian living. It is important for this audience to know that you respect their experience in life, their ability to read and understand Bible stories, and their interest in making a positive difference in their lives. It is also important for them to know that you do not expect them to be biblical scholars.

Working with the Adult Learner

Adult learners bring a variety of learning styles, experiences, gifts, and questions to the Bible study. Everyone in the group, both learners and leader, has something to offer to other individuals and to the group. It is important for the leader to recognize and respect the diversity of experience and opinion that exists in a group of adult learners. There will not always be agreement or consensus. The leader may find that living with the questions is more important than finding the right answers. Helping the learner to search for better questions and share personal insights is often more productive than looking for answers.

As beginners in adult Bible study, the learners also bring many insecurities and uncertainties about their ability to participate successfully. The questions and activities in the resource help learners explore the biblical material as it connects with their experiences. One of the goals of this course is to help learners become more confident in their ability to read and understand the Bible. Most adults who participate in this basic Bible course will quickly gain the skills and confidence necessary to participate in a more in-depth level of study as they seek to learn how to respond to their call to follow Jesus.

Needs of adult learners

Adults are motivated to participate in Bible study by a diverse set of interests and questions. Kent Johnson, a professor of Christian education, suggests that coping with transitions is the single most common motivating factor (*Developing Skills for Teaching Adults,* Teaching the Faith Participant Guide, [Minneapolis: Augsburg Fortress, 1993], 6f). Adults are all, however, seeking enrichment, growth, and ways to make a positive difference in their lives and the lives of others.

Leaders need to recognize the varying needs of the adult learners in their groups. Michael Sack identifies four distinct adult audiences in our churches today. Each generation, according to Sack, has its own identity and needs:

Generation X includes adults who are 16 to 25 years old. They battle low self-esteem and gather in small groups of their peers for support and nurture. They turn to the church for unconditional acceptance and to hear a message of hope.

Busters are 25 to 35 years old. They are firmly grounded and can provide strong leadership for the church. They need relationships, to talk things over with their peers, and to work for a better world.

Boomers are 35 to 50 years old. They look to faith in Christ for a stabilizing influence. They need to discuss meaning, self-definition, and worth.

Older adults are 50 and up. They possess skills and want to do something worthwhile. They need to be appreciated for their experience, insight, and abilities.

This is one way to demonstrate the diversity among adult learners. It is important to recognize that within each of these groups there are individuals who struggle with personal issues. In the course of this study, each individual needs to be heard, respected, and affirmed.

(From *Brain Scan of America* by Michael Sack, copyright © 1995 Michael C. Sack, Cultural Insights, Inc.)

Learning styles

Adult learners have different learning styles. This has to do with how they prefer to encounter and act upon new insights and information. Some adults sit quietly, watching and listening to the group before drawing their own conclusions. Others appreciate the opportunity to do a skit or play a role to express their thoughts and feelings. Some prefer a presentation followed by a question-and-answer period. Others show little interest in group solutions, preferring to act as individuals on practical problems.

To help the leader accommodate the various learning styles of the adult learner, this resource presents two biblical texts—brief segments in the learner book that put the texts into their biblical context—and activities that encourage learning through asking, telling, doing, and imagining. The leader should select activities that guide the participants in a dialogue with the text at all levels—thinking, feeling, intuition, and experience.

Course Introduction

THIS COURSE WILL HELP YOU and the learner become acquainted with ten significant events in the life of Jesus: Jesus' birth, Jesus' baptism, the temptation of Jesus in the wilderness, the cleansing of the temple, the Sermon on the Mount, the healing of the paralytic, the Last Supper, the crucifixion, the road to Emmaus, and the ascension.

Those ten significant events are combined to form five sessions of study. The sixth session provides a review for the participants in the study.

1. A New Beginning. The learners discover that through Jesus' birth and Jesus' baptism, God has become one with humankind.

2. Beyond the Limits. The learners discover that God will give them the strength to be faithful in times of trial and temptation.

3. Outside the Circle. This session focuses on God who blesses people who least expect to be blessed.

4. Given and Shed for You . This session reminds the learners that at the table and on the cross, Jesus gave his life for them.

5. After We Say Good-bye. The learners discover that it was necessary for Jesus to leave so that his work and his ministry might continue.

6. More than Just Details. This session helps the learners draw the conclusion that their relationship with God in Jesus Christ gives them life and is the primary focus of their lives.

We have attempted to help make the life and the stories of Jesus come alive, and hopefully, through the expansion of these stories help the participants see that studying the Bible can be exciting and fun. Also, we hope that as the participants of this study finish, they will be encouraged to continue to read the Bible; and discover, through their reading the joy, comfort, and strength, of knowing that the stories of their lives intersect with the stories of Jesus' at the crossroads of the biblical texts.

As the participants experience life at these crossroads, we hope they will gain further insight into these questions: What does the biblical text tell me about God? What does the biblical text tell me about the people of God? What does this text say about me?

As the participants begin to deal with these questions, we trust that they will be given new strength as they live out their lives at the crossroads. We also hope that the participants will trust that as they journey throughout their lives, God in God's son Jesus the Christ continues to journey with them.

That God is with them as they experience new beginnings, when they are tempted, when they feel left out or alone, when they celebrate the Lord's Supper or think about the Lord's suffering and death, when they are forced to say good-bye to their friends and loved ones as they continue their journey of life alone.

May God bless you as you study!

Course Objectives

This course will help the learners:
- learn basic stories about the life and ministry of Jesus;
- recognize Jesus as Son of the Living God and Savior of the world;
- see themselves as children of God who discover, in Jesus, hope and meaning for their daily lives.

① A New Beginning

God declares oneness with humankind.

Luke 2:1-20 The Birth of Jesus
Matthew 3:13-17 The Baptism of Jesus

Gathering

☐ Use the "We're in This Together" strategy (page 20 of the leader guide). Have the learners share their birth stories or their adoption stories.

● ● ● ● ● ● ● ● ● ● ● ● ● ● ● ● ● ● ●

Luke 2:1-20
The Birth of Jesus

Read the Story

☐ Have learners read the story of Jesus' birth from Luke 2:1-20. Consider using the "Reading Partners" strategy (page 20 of the leader guide).

Expand the Story

☐ Have the learners read "I Can't Believe This Is Happening" (page 3 of the learner book). Use the "Each One Share One" strategy (page 20 of the leader guide) and have the learners respond to the following:

- If you were to pick a way for God's son to enter the world, which way would you choose?
- If you were Joseph, how might you have felt about all that was happening?
- The message of the angels said, "To you is born this day in the city of David, a savior…" How is this birth for you?
- Write what Mary would have written in her diary for the day of Jesus' birth.

☐ Have the learners retell the story in the form of a newscast. Use the "More Heads Are Better Than One" strategy (page 20 of the leader guide).

☐ Have the learners develop a birth announcement that would be sent from Joseph and Mary, announcing the birth of Jesus. Use the "Wherever Three or Four" strategy (page 20 of the leader guide).

● ● ● ● ● ● ● ● ● ● ● ● ● ● ● ● ● ● ●

Matthew 3:13-17
The Baptism of Jesus

Read the Story

☐ Using the "Moment of Solitude" strategy (page 21 of the leader guide), have the learners read the story of the baptism of Jesus, Matthew 3:13-17 in the NRSV Bible. Suggest the following questions to help guide their reflection on the text: What does the biblical text tell me about God? What does the biblical text tell me about the people of God? What does this text say about me?

Expand the Story

☐ Read John's story "But I Don't Want To!" (page 6 of the learner book). Use the "Wherever Three or Four" strategy (page 20 of the leader guide).

☐ Answer these questions using the "Who's Ready?" strategy (page 20 of the leader guide):

- Why do you believe Jesus needed to be baptized by John?
- Why does John at first hesitate to baptize Jesus?
- The voice from heaven says, "This is my Son, the Beloved." In your baptism, what did God say to you?

☐ Ask the learners if they can share anything they know or remember about their baptismal day. Use the "Each One Share One" strategy (page 20 of the leader guide).

☐ Have the learners finish the following story that begins: "I was there that day when Jesus was baptized, and I…" Use the "Moment of Solitude" strategy (page 21 of the leader guide).

☐ Have the learners plan a baptismal birthday celebration for the following week. Use the "We're in This Together" strategy (page 20 of the leader guide).

● ●

Focus the Stories

☐ Read the story "Never Alone" (page 9 of the learner book). You might use the "Let's Role-Play" strategy (page 21 of the leader guide). Allow some time for the learners to write some notes in response to the questions on page 10 of the learner book (the questions are also included below). Invite the learners to discuss the questions using the "Teaching Twosome" strategy (page 21 of the leader guide).

- What does it mean to be born or adopted into your family?
- What does it mean to be born or adopted into God's family?
- What are some ways that you have experienced the family of God because of your baptism into the body of Christ?
- How have you experienced God's presence in your life?
- If you were Billy's mom, what would you have said to Billy about baptism?

☐ Use the "Teaching Twosome" strategy (page 21 of the leader guide) to discuss the question: If you were to explain the significance of your baptism to a friend who was not baptized, what would you say that would help your friend see its significance?

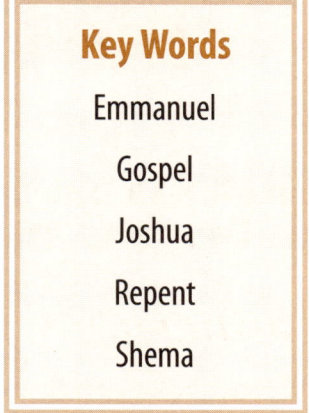

Key Words

Emmanuel

Gospel

Joshua

Repent

Shema

Leaders note: Baptism is a sign of God's grace. It is a sacrament in which God accepts the individual without anything required in return. Baptism is also a rite of initiation into the family of God. Finally, baptism is a daily participation in the death and resurrection of Jesus Christ, in which the believer is called to continue to walk in God's grace.

☐ Have the learners write a letter as a parent might write to their child expressing their hope for their child on the day of their birth—the day of their baptism. Use the "Moment of Solitude" strategy (page 21 of the leader guide).

Closing

☐ Close by singing a familiar Christmas hymn.

2 Beyond the Limits

God gives the church and us the strength to be faithful in the midst of temptation.

Luke 4:1-13 The Temptation of Jesus
Mark 11:15-19 The Cleansing of the Temple

Gathering

☐ Have the learners share their highs and lows for the week. Use the "Who's Ready?" strategy (page 20 of the leader guide).

Luke 4:1-13
The Temptation of Jesus

Read the Story

☐ Have the learners read the story of the temptation of Jesus from Luke 4:1-13. Use the "Moment of Solitude" strategy (page 21 of the leader guide).

Expand the Story

☐ Have the learners read "Attack in the Wilderness" (page 11 of the learner book). Use the "Let's Role-Play" strategy" (page 21 of the leader guide) to dramatize the story or the learners' reaction to the story.

☐ Have the learners answer the following questions using the "Teaching Twosome" strategy (page 21 of the leader guide).

- Satan's attack on Jesus hits him at his most vulnerable points: food, power, the temptation to worship someone other than God. If the attack were to take place on you in a wilderness in today's society, what would be your most vulnerable points?

- God's presence helps Jesus remain faithful in the midst of temptation. How does God help us when we are faced with temptation?

- The sixth petition of the Lord's Prayer, "Lead us not into temptation" has also been translated, "Save us from the time of trial." Can you share some specific times when you have felt tempted, and successfully have resisted that temptation?

☐ Invite the learners to create ads that could have been used by Satan in the wilderness. Use the "Brainstorm" strategy (page 21 of the leader guide).

Mark 11:15-19
The Cleansing of the Temple

Read the Story

☐ Have the learners read the story of the temple cleansing from Mark 11:15-19. Use the "Reading Partners" strategy (page 20 of the leader guide).

☐ Distribute copies of the "Interior of the Temple in Jerusalem" reproducible page (page 23 of the leader guide). This handout and the diagram of the temple in the learner book (page 15) will help learners understand the references to the temple. The priests conducted ritual sacrifices in the Court of the Priests. Only Israelites were allowed in the interior of the temple. The men could watch from the Court of the Israelites. The women watched through the gate between the two rooms. The Gentiles could gather outside the inner precincts. It is in the Court of the Gentiles that Jesus encounters the buyers and sellers.

Expand the Story

☐ Read the story "I Was There" (page 14 of the learner book). Use the "We're in This Together" strategy (page 20 of the leader guide) and invite the learners to answer these questions:

- What was it about the practices of those who were buying and selling in the temple that made Jesus' anger justified?
- In turn, why were the chief priests afraid after the incident?
- Do you see any relationship between what was going on in the temple in Jesus' day with what is happening in many churches today?

☐ Use the "We're in This Together" strategy (page 20 of the leader guide) and invite the learners to complete this sentence: "The greatest temptation for the church today is…"

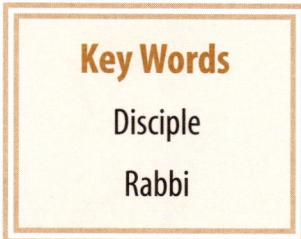

Key Words

Disciple

Rabbi

Focus the Stories

☐ Use the "Teaching Twosome" strategy (page 21 of the leader guide) to help the learners respond to and discuss the "In the Hour of Trial" questions (page 17 of the learner book).

☐ Give the learners the following assignment: There are pastoral candidates who will be interviewed by a call committee of St. John's Church and are asked the following question: "Pastor, it really concerns me that our church has become a business and all we care about at this church is balancing our budget. What can we do as a church to prevent that from happening?" You may want to use the "More Heads Are Better Than One" strategy (page 20 of the leader guide).

☐ Ask the learners to write a personal prayer that they can use to help them in the times when they are tempted or tested. The "Moment of Solitude" strategy (page 21 of the leader guide) may be helpful in this activity. There is space in the learner book to record this prayer (page 18 of the learner book).

☐ Invite the learners to think about a particular person or some people they know that may be facing a temptation. Ask the learners what they might do to support these people in their hour of trial. (Note: remind the learners to respect confidentiality so that what is said during the discussion is not repeated outside the discussion.) You may want to use the "We're in This Together" strategy (page 20 of the leader guide).

Closing

☐ Close by asking the learners to write prayers of thanksgiving for the ways in which God has helped them in their moments of trials or temptations. Use the "Moment of Solitude" strategy (page 21 of the leader guide). There is space in the learner book to record this prayer (page 18 of the learner book).

3 Outside the Circle

The blessing of God continues for those who may least expect to be blessed.

Matthew 5:1-12 The Sermon on the Mount
Mark 2:1-12 The Healing of the Paralytic

Gathering

☐ Invite the learners to share one blessing that has been important in their lives. Use the "Each One Share One" strategy (page 20 of the leader guide).

• • • • • • • • • • • • • • • • • • • •

Matthew 5:1-12
The Sermon on the Mount

Read the Story

☐ Have the learners read the story of the Beatitudes from Matthew 5:1-12. Use the "Reading Partners" strategy (page 20 of the leader guide).

Expand the Story

☐ Have the learners read "A Memorable Sermon" (page 19 of the learner book). Use the "Moment of Solitude" strategy (page 21 of the leader guide). Suggest the following questions to help guide their reflection on the text: What does the biblical text tell me about God? What does the biblical text tell me about the people of God? What does this text say about me?

☐ Have the learners respond to these questions using the "Each One Share One" strategy (page 20 of the leader guide).

• How did Miriam see women outside the circle of society in Jesus' day?

• What did it mean to be blessed in Jesus' day? What does it mean today?

• As Jesus began the Sermon on the Mount, he sat down. What does Jesus' sitting down symbolize?

• In the beginning of the sermon, Jesus talks about people who are displaced or outside the circle of the mainstream of society. When have you experienced life outside the circle?

• How have you been blessed by God?

☐ Have the learners make a list of people they could bless, and how they could bless them. Use the "Brainstorm" strategy (page 21 of the leader guide).

• • • • • • • • • • • • • • • • • • • •

Mark 2:1-12
The Healing of the Paralytic

Read the Story

☐ Have the learners read the story of the healing of the paralytic from Mark 2:1-12. Use the "Who's Ready?" strategy (page 20 of the leader guide) to gather as many responses as possible in three or four minutes to the basic questions of this study: What does the biblical text tell me about God? What does the biblical text tell me about the people of God? What does this text say about me?

Expand the Story

☐ Use the "Let's Role-Play" strategy (page 21 of the leader guide) to read "It Was a Miracle" (page 22 of the learner book). Then use the "Teaching Two-some" strategy (page 21 of the leader guide) as the learners consider the following questions:

• Jesus praises the paralytic for his great faith. What made the paralytic's faith so great?

• The forgiveness of the paralytic's sins comes before the healing. Why? (Note: Often illness and sin were connected in the Bible. However, there is no direct evidence that this is the case here.)

• Think of loved ones who have been ill or times that you have been ill. How has God's healing been a present force in the midst of that illness?

□ Use the "Moment of Solitude" strategy (page 21 of the leader guide). Have the learners think about relationships that may need healing. Have them write down what they believe needs to be done, fold it, and put it in a safe place. Encourage them to pray about it every day between sessions.

Focus the Stories

□ Ask a volunteer to read the story, "Pray for My Healing" (page 29 of the learner book). Discuss the following questions using the "Each One Share One" strategy (page 20 of the leader guide). (These questions also appear on page 30 of the learner book.)

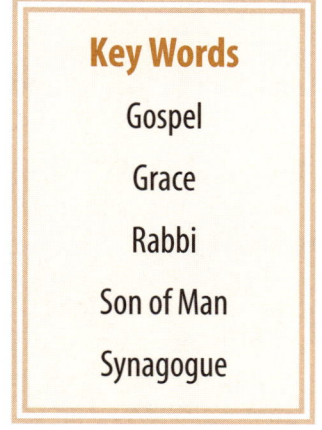

Key Words

Gospel

Grace

Rabbi

Son of Man

Synagogue

- What prayer would you pray if you were Rosalyn?

- If you prayed for healing and it was clear that healing was not going to happen, what would you say to your friend?

- Sarah says, "I know I've been forgiven…this illness has nothing to do with my sin." How would you respond to her statement?

- How does God heal in today's world? (Keep in mind that the word for *healing* and *salvation* are the same word in Greek.)

□ Have the learners describe a time in their lives when they believed they were outside the circle. Who brought them into the circle? What has God done to bring people into the circle of God's kingdom? (God has given us Jesus Christ to suffer and die so we might be reunited with God.) Use the "Each One Share One" strategy (page 20 of the leader guide).

□ Invite the learners to imagine that as lawyers, they are called to defend a Jehovah's Witness family who refuses to give their son a blood transfusion without which he will die. What is their defense? Use the "Brainstorm" strategy (page 21 of the leader guide).

Closing

□ Distribute copies of the hymn "Guide Me Ever Great Redeemer" (page 22 of the leader guide). Have the learners read or sing the first verse of the hymn. Use the "We're in This Together" strategy (page 20 of the leader guide).

④ Given and Shed for You

At the table, on the cross, Jesus gave his life for me.

Matthew 26:17-30 The Lord's Supper
Mark 15:21-39 The Crucifixion

Gathering

☐ Have learners describe a memorable meal they participated in. Use the "Who's Ready?" strategy (page 20 of the leader guide) as you share stories.

☐ Distribute copies of the "Map of Jerusalem at the Time of Jesus' Crucifixion" (page 24 of the leader guide) and "Events in Holy Week" (page 25 of the leader guide). These reproducible pages provide an overview of the events in Holy Week.

• • • • • • • • • • • • • • • • • • • •

Matthew 26:17-30
The Lord's Supper

Read the Story

☐ Have learners read the story of the Lord's Supper from Matthew 26:17-30. Use the "Moment of Solitude" strategy (page 21 of the leader guide) to reflect on the questions: What does the biblical text tell me about God? What does the biblical text tell me about the people of God? What does this text say about me?

Expand the Story

☐ Use the "Let's Role-Play" strategy (page 21 of the leader guide). Have the learners read "Remember When?" (page 31 of the learner book). Invite the learners to answer these questions using the "Study Buddies" strategy (page 21 of the leader guide).

• What meal were the disciples celebrating when the Lord's Supper was observed?

• What benefits did the disciples receive from the Lord's Supper?

• Who was it that left the supper early in order to lead the Roman soldiers to arrest Jesus?

• What benefits do you receive from your participation in the Lord's Supper?

☐ The word *Eucharist* is another word of communion which means "thanksgiving." Have the learners make a list of the things and the people for which they are thankful. Use the "Teaching Twosome" strategy (page 21 of the leader guide) as you share responses.

☐ Have the learners share stories of their first communion. Use the "Each One Share One" strategy (page 20 of the leader guide).

• • • • • • • • • • • • • • • • • • • •

Mark 15:21-39
The Crucifixion

Read the Story

☐ Have the learners read the story of the crucifixion from Mark 15:21-39. Use the "Reading Partners" strategy (page 20 of the leader guide).

Expand the Story

☐ Ask a volunteer to read the story, "He Was the Son of God" (page 34 of the learner book). Have the learners answer these questions using the "Wherever Three or Four" strategy (page 20 of the leader guide).

• Jesus died on Good Friday. Why do we call it good?

• Jesus' death on the cross is considered a moment of triumph. Why?

• The centurion had become indifferent to suffering and death on the cross. Why was Jesus' death significant for him? What difference did Jesus' death make to the centurion?

- What difference does Jesus' death make to you? In how you live? In how you approach death?

☐ Use the "Before and After" strategy (page 21 of the leader guide) to explore the ideas and feelings learners have about death and funerals. Invite the learners to visit, as a class, a cemetery or funeral home. Have the learners talk about their feelings regarding cemeteries and funerals.

☐ Use the "Moment of Solitude" strategy (page 21 of the leader guide) and invite the learners to write their own epitaph.

Focus the Stories

☐ Read the section, "And in the End" (pages 37 and 38 of the learner book). Discuss the learners' responses to the questions using the "Each One Share One" strategy (page 20 of the leader guide).

Key Words

Blasphemy

Centurion

Gospel

Passover

Sanhedrin

Son of God

Theophilus

☐ Stage a discussion over the question: Does death come as an enemy or does death come as a friend?

Begin by using the "Where Do You Stand" strategy (page 21 of the leader guide). If you wish to have a debate, have the learner choose opposing sides between enemy and friend. If you wish to have a discussion, use a continuum with one side of the room being enemy, and the other side being friend. Learners may stand anywhere on or between the extremes.

☐ Use the "Before and After" strategy (page 21 of the leader guide) and ask an oncology nurse or a hospice volunteer to share how they believe their Christian faith helps them deal with death and those who are dying.

☐ Invite the learners to plan their own funeral service. Begin with a discussion of funeral services the learners have attended. The learner book provides some direction and space for this activity (page 38 of the learner book). Then use the "Study Buddies" strategy (page 21 of the leader guide) as the learners plan their funeral service. Include the hymns, the possible Bible texts, solo music selections, and pall bearers. Remember that the function of the funeral service is twofold: to teach what the church believes about death; and to create an environment in which it is possible to say good-bye to the deceased friend or loved one. The funeral service from your book of worship is a good resource for this activity.

Closing

☐ Have the learners pick a favorite hymn that helps them deal with death, and then suggest that the class sing or read one of the hymns as a closing prayer.

5 After We Say Good-bye

It was necessary for Jesus to leave for the ministry of the kingdom to begin.

Luke 24:13-35 The Road to Emmaus
Acts 1:6-11 The Ascension

Gathering

☐ Use the "Each One Share One" strategy (page 20 of the leader guide) and have the learners describe a difficult good-bye with a friend or loved one.

● ●

Luke 24:13-35
The Road to Emmaus

Read the Story

☐ Use the "Reading Partners" strategy (page 20 of the leader guide) and have the learners read the story of the road to Emmaus from Luke 24:13-35.

Expand the Story

☐ Have the learners read "Jesus Appears on the Road" (page 39 of the learner book). Use the "Teaching Twosome" strategy (page 21 of the leader guide) and have the learners respond to these questions:

- Elizabeth Kubler-Ross has outlined five stages of grief: denial, anger, bargaining, depression, and acceptance. As the story begins, what stage(s) best describe what Cleopas is experiencing?

- If you were on the road that day with Cleopas, how might you have reacted to Jesus' sudden appearance?

- Have the learners share a time when they received unexpected, but welcomed, guests in their home.

☐ Emmaus is a place of discovery for Cleopas and his friend. Have the learners share important discoveries they have made. Use the "Who's Ready?" strategy (page 20 of the leader guide) to gather responses.

● ●

Acts 1:6-11
The Ascension

Read the Story

☐ Use the "Moment of Solitude" strategy (page 21 of the leader guide). Have the learners read the story of the ascension of Jesus from Acts 1:6-11. Suggest the following questions to help guide their reflection on the text: What does the biblical text tell me about God? What does the biblical text tell me about the people of God? What does this text say about me?

Expand the Story

☐ Ask a volunteer to read the story, "We Never Got a Chance to Say Good-bye" (page 42 of the learner book). Use the "Study Buddies" strategy (page 21 of the leader guide) to respond to the following questions:

- The disciples ask, "Is this the time when you will restore the kingdom to Israel?" What did the disciples expect from Jesus?

- Do you believe that Jesus' leaving meant that Jesus had confidence in the ability of his disciples to carry on his mission?

- What skills or power has God given to today's church to continue Jesus' mission here on earth?

- How has God helped you be a part of the continuation of that mission?

☐ Let's talk about it. Organize a debate that focuses on the topic: "Good-byes are difficult and if people want to avoid them, it's all right." Use the "Where

Do You Stand?" strategy (page 21 of the leader guide) followed by the "Wherever Three or Four" strategy (page 20 of the leader guide).

Focus the Stories

☐ Read the story "Good-byes Are Always Difficult" (page 45 of the learner book). Use the "Study Buddies" strategy (page 21 of the leader guide) to discuss the following questions:

Key Words

Disciple

Gospel

Messiah

Rabbi

Theophilus

- How does God give you strength to remain faithful to your calling and faithful to your Lord, even when you face good-byes?

- How can your faith help you as you approach the task of saying good-bye?

- What strength, if any, can you find in saying good-bye?

☐ Use the "We're in This Together" strategy (page 20 of the leader guide) and invite learners to remember times at various stages in their lives when they said good-bye and to complete the chart (page 46 of the learner book).

☐ Invite the learners to write a letter to their loved ones that is to be opened at the time of their death. What would they say? How would they say good-bye? Use the "Who's Ready?" strategy (page 20 of the leader guide) to allow the learners to share.

☐ Share with the learners that the word *good-bye* comes from an Old English word that means "God be with you!" Then ask them to share a time when God's presence strengthened them during a time when they were forced to say good-bye. Use the "Each One Share One" strategy (page 20 of the leader guide).

☐ The disciples were strengthened on the day of Pentecost, some ten days after the ascension to continue Jesus' mission. Ask the learners to share a time when they believed they received strength from God to continue on, after a difficult good-bye. Use the "Study Buddies" strategy (page 21 of the leader guide).

Closing

☐ Close with a hymn such as "Eternal Father, Strong to Save."

6 More Than Just Details

My relationship with God in Jesus Christ gives me life.

John 14:6 Review and Summary

Gathering

☐ Have the learners finish this phrase: God's gift of life helps me… Use the "Brainstorm" strategy (page 21 of the leader guide).

● ● ● ● ● ● ● ● ● ● ● ● ● ● ● ● ● ● ●

John 14:6
Review and Summary

Read the Story

☐ Have the learners read John 14:6. Use the "Who's Ready?" strategy (page 20 of the leader guide) and the following questions to guide reflection on the text: What does the biblical text tell me about God? What does the biblical text tell me about the people of God? What does this text say about me?

Expand the Story

☐ Have the learners read Thomas's story, "To Those Who Have Not Seen" (page 47 of the learner book). If the learners are not familiar with the story of Thomas, ask them to read John 20:19-29.

☐ Have the learners discuss the following questions using the "Wherever Three or Four" strategy (page 20 of the leader guide).

• What does Thomas's story mean to me?

• How does the life of which Thomas speaks empower me, or give me hope?

• Thomas refers to John's close of the Gospel when he says that we who have not seen and yet believe are blessed. How have you been blessed?

—By Jesus' birth?

—Through your baptism?

—As you are tempted?

—As you face death?

—As you share in the Lord's Supper?

—When you think about your participation in Christ's mission on earth?

• As you think about the above situations, how does your relationship with God and God's people give you hope?

• How does your relationship with God and God's people give you joy?

Focus the Story

☐ Have the learners read the story "What Is Life?" (page 48 of the learner book). Use the "Moment of Solitude" strategy (page 21 of the leader guide) to respond to the questions that follow the story.

☐ Invite the learners to make a list of the top ten priorities that they have in their lives. Ask them to rank the priorities in order of importance with one being the most important and ten being the least important. Use the "Who's Ready?" strategy (page 20 of the leader guide) as you ask the learners to respond to the following questions:

• What are the areas of your life that give you the least satisfaction? What could you do to change those areas?

• What are the areas of your life that give you the greatest satisfaction? Share why they are so satisfying.

• As you survey the various aspects of your life, how do you see God at work as you experience those aspects of your life?

• As you think about the areas you have listed, how does your membership in the family of God help your faith grow?

• As you think about the areas of your life that you have listed and prioritized, how does your relationship with God help you as you live your life in those areas?

- A T-shirt says, "Soccer is Life…the rest is just details!" From the perspective of your Christian faith and what you have learned from this study, how would you rewrite that slogan?
- Have the learners discuss the following summary questions using the "Study Buddies" strategy (page 21 of the leader guide).

☐ In one sentence or phrase, share what you learned about the following stories:
- The birth of Jesus.
- The baptism of Jesus.
- The temptation of Jesus in the wilderness.
- The cleansing of the temple.
- The Sermon on the Mount.
- The healing of the paralytic.
- The Last Supper.
- The crucifixion.
- The road to Emmaus.
- The ascension.

☐ As I participated in this study I discovered that studying the Bible
- still remains as much of a mystery as it ever was.
- is not as intimidating as I thought it would be.
- is something I want to continue.
- was a nice experience, but I don't have time for anything more.

☐ Have the learners discuss the following questions using the "Brainstorm" strategy (page 21 of the leader guide).
- How would you respond if a friend were to ask you, "Why should I study the Bible?"
- What hope, joy, or comfort have you discovered from participating in this study?

Closing

☐ Close with a prayer of thanksgiving, thanking God for this experience.

Discussion Strategies

We're in This Together

Learners work in groups of two and then combine with another group of two to share their thoughts and insights. During this time, the leader moves about the room to observe the progress of each group. Then the groups of four report to the whole group.

Reading Partners

Invite learners to pick a reading partner for the six sessions. If you have an uneven number of learners, assign three to one group.

Each reading pair is responsible for reading from the learner book and the Bible as assigned. Each pair can decide for themselves who will read when and how much. (It might happen, for example, that in some pairs one person does all the reading. Ideally, each partner will take a turn.)

Who's Ready?

In this discussion technique, the learners choose for themselves when they are ready to respond. You might say, "Let's discuss these questions. Who would like to begin?"

The advantage of this strategy is that the learners can respond when they are ready. The leader will have the responsibility to involve those who are less likely to volunteer.

Each One Share One

In groups of three or four, learners take turns sharing thoughts about the question or issue. In doing so, learners need to know that their thoughts and their opinions are valid and will be affirmed. Others in the group are not to argue or debate during this activity. This strategy can be used to build trust levels within the classroom.

More Heads Are Better Than One

A question is asked, and then the learners work together in groups of three or four to reach a consensus and develop a common answer, which is then shared with the larger group. Consensus is reached when all members agree or can, at least, live with the answer offered.

In this strategy, one person in each small group must act as moderator. The moderator makes certain that all members speak and are not interrupted, restates major points of the discussion, helps the group form a consensus statement, makes sure everyone comes to accept the statement through votes or other methods, and shares the group's work with the whole group.

As you use this strategy throughout the course, invite different people to be the moderator. It is helpful to choose those whom you feel will do a good job at this initially so they can serve as good role models, but everyone should have the opportunity to play this role. You can help learners be successful in this role by roaming from group to group, listening in, and offering positive comments or gentle guidance.

This strategy helps the learners value the process of consensus-building. It allows them to learn how to negotiate between different ideas, and yet it enables them to see the similarities present in the midst of their differences. It also demonstrates the importance of the involvement of the faith community in biblical interpretation.

Wherever Three or Four

Learners work in groups of three or four for the purpose of discussing a question or working cooperatively to complete a poster, collage, or other activity. This is helpful for not only small group work, but it teaches learners that Christ's presence is at work in the smallest groups.

Moment of Solitude

Learners work silently in a corner of the room or in separate areas of the building to either read an assignment, master a task, write a report, memorize a section of scripture, or write reflections in a journal. Then learners return to class and share insights from their solitude. This is a somewhat different "discussion" strategy in that sometimes the discussion is not with the class but with God.

The advantage of this strategy is that it cuts down on distractions and helps the learners begin to deal with their personal thoughts and feelings. Allow time for sharing thoughts and insights in the larger group. Learners should share only what they are comfortable having the group know.

Let's Role-Play

The learners are divided into groups that reflect the number of players the situation demands. They are then told to act out the situation to a resolution or simply to act out a scene or Bible story. They can also be asked to create their own role-play to address particular issues or Bible stories.

If role-plays are used, it is helpful to remember that:
- not all learners are comfortable speaking in front of their peers. These learners can be very valuable in writing scripts and offering ideas, however;
- a time limit for the preparation of role-plays needs to be closely followed;
- it may be beneficial to assign a role-play to a group of learners in advance for presentation the following week;
- the primary purpose of a role-play is to help the learners identify more closely with a situation or story.

Teaching Twosome

Learners work on their own; then they find a partner and share with that partner. The strategy emphasizes that as individuals learn, they also teach; and that you can learn from each other. It is not necessary that reports be made to the entire group.

Study Buddies

Have the learners choose a partner with whom they will work on answering the questions that have been assigned.

Brainstorm

Learners work individually within a group of three or four, writing the first thought related to the issue to be discussed and then sharing that thought with the rest of the group.

When using this strategy, it is helpful to remember these guidelines:
- all ideas are accepted;
- variety is encouraged;
- ideas are not to be evaluated or ranked;
- ideas need not be defined;
- a time limit is set.

This strategy helps learners gain the confidence that their opinions are valued and do not necessarily have to be backed with lots of facts or align with the opinions of others.

Before and After

Learners work together in groups of two or three. Before reading a story, hearing a speaker, researching an issue, participating in a field trip, and so forth, learners share what they know or feel and then develop questions about the topic.

After the experience, the small group reconvenes to share what they have learned or discovered about the topic.

Where Do You Stand?

On any given question, point to different spots in the room. If the question is agree/disagree or true/false, one side of the room would be agree or true and the other side of the room would be disagree or false. If the question entails a ranking, such as 1 to 10, have the learners arrange themselves on the continuum according to where they stand on the issue.

The benefit of this strategy is that it visually reminds the learners that to have an opinion means to take a stand or a position about a certain issue.

The discussion that follows can be a debate between individuals with opposing opinions, or simply a time for each individual to share why they chose to stand where they did.

Guide Me Ever, Great Redeemer

Guide me ever, great Redeemer,
Pilgrim through this barren land.
I am weak, but you are mighty;
Hold me with your powerful hand.
Bread of heaven, bread of heaven,
Feed me now and evermore,
Feed me now and evermore.

Open now the crystal fountain
Where the healing waters flow;
Let the fire and cloudy pillar
Lead me all my journey through.
Strong deliverer, strong deliverer,
Shield me with your mighty arm,
Shield me with your mighty arm.

When I tread the verge of Jordan,
Bid my anxious fears subside;
Death of death and hell's destruction,
Land me safe on Canaan's side.
Songs and praises, songs and praises,
I will raise forever more,
I will raise forever more.

(*Lutheran Book of Worship* 343)

Interior of the Temple in Jerusalem

Court of the Priests

Sanctuary **Altar** **Court of the Israelites** **Court of the Priests**

Court of the Gentiles

Court of the Women

Map of Jerusalem at the Time of Jesus' Crucifixion

This map is to be used with "Events in Holy Week."

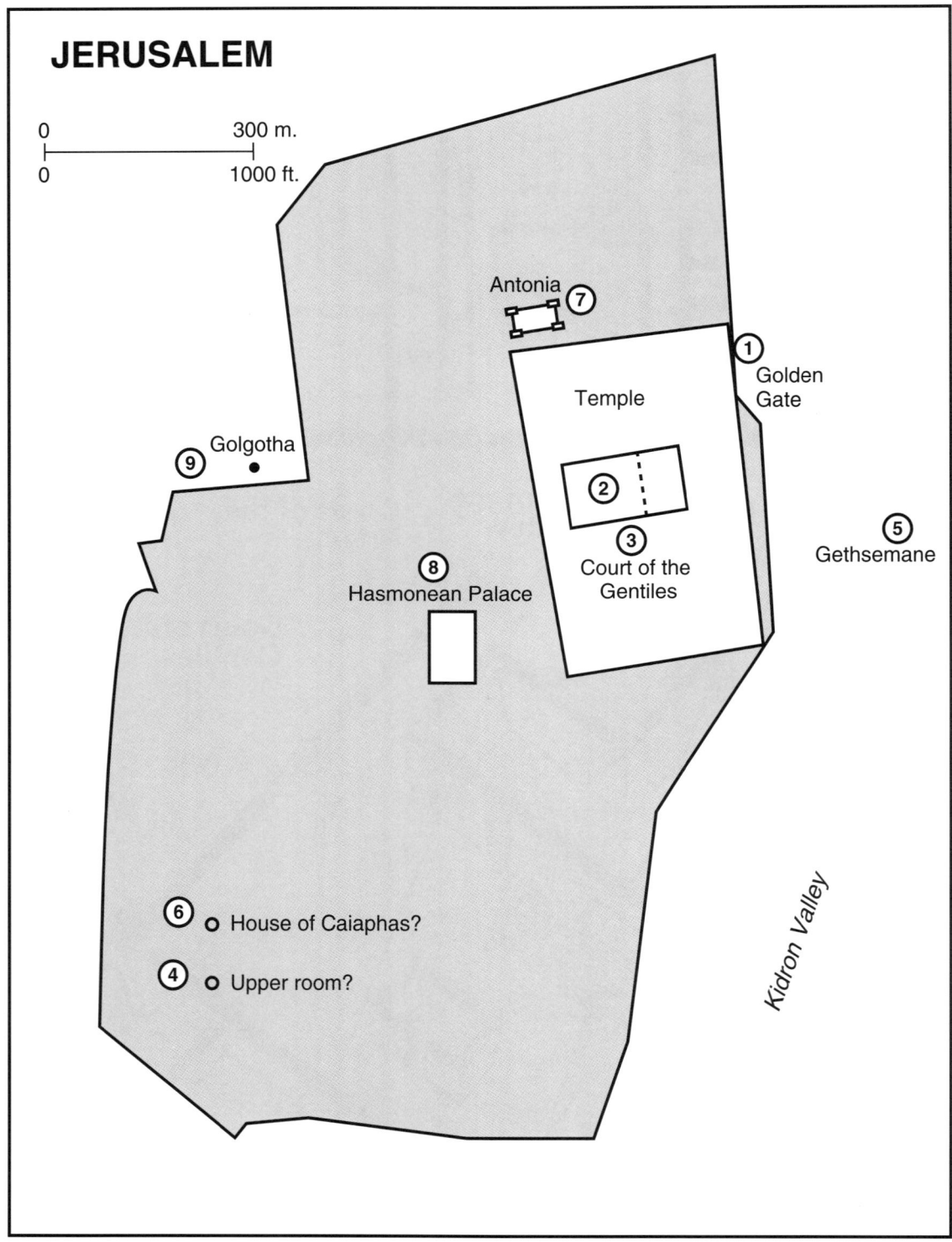

JERUSALEM

0   300 m.

0   1000 ft.

Antonia ⑦

① Golden Gate

Temple

Golgotha

⑨ •

②

③

Court of the Gentiles

⑤

Gethsemane

⑧

Hasmonean Palace

Kidron Valley

⑥ ○ House of Caiaphas?

④ ○ Upper room?

Events in Holy Week

The following information is to be used with the "Map of Jerusalem at the Time of Jesus' Crucifixion."

WHILE SCHOLARS DISAGREE about the exact location of the events during the week prior to Jesus' death and resurrection, this map and the following narrative present one likely scenario.

1. On Palm Sunday Jesus makes a triumphal entry into Jerusalem through the Golden Gate. The expectation on this day of a new king like David stands in stark contrast to Jesus being crucified as "King of the Jews" (Mark 11:1-10).

2. Following the triumphal entry Jesus makes a brief visit to the temple, probably to the Court of Israel where only men were allowed. It was late in the day so Jesus and his disciples traveled the short distance to Bethany where they spent the night (Mark 11:11).

3. The following day, Jesus returns to the temple and drives out the sellers of sacrificial animals from the Court of the Gentiles. This court is the area outside the inner precincts. Jews and Gentiles were welcome here (Mark 11:15-19).

4. Jesus celebrates the Last Supper in an upper room of a house in Jerusalem. The exact location of the upper room is not known (Mark 14:12-25).

5. Following the Last Supper, Jesus and his disciples leave the city to pray in a place called Gethsemane. Gethsemane is located in the Kidron Valley, east of Jerusalem. It is here that Jesus is arrested (Mark 14:26-52).

6. Following his arrest, Jesus is taken to the house of Caiaphas, the high priest. Peter follows Jesus and it is in the courtyard that Peter denies any association with Jesus (Mark 14:53-72).

7. Jesus then appears before Pontius Pilate, the Roman governor of Judea, Samaria, and Idumaea. This encounter may have taken place at the fortress Antonia located at the northwest corner of the temple area. The location of the fortress allowed the Romans to keep an eye on the activity at the temple (Mark 15:1-15).

8. Jesus' appearance before Herod is recorded only in the Gospel of Luke (Luke 23:6-12).

9. Jesus is then led through the narrow streets of Jerusalem. The condemned were forced to carry their own cross through the streets in an effort to publicly humiliate the criminal. Jesus is unable to carry his cross, so Simon of Cyrene is compelled to carry the cross to a place outside the city wall called Golgotha where Jesus is crucified (Mark 15:21-32).

Bible Study Resources

AS YOU READ THE BIBLE, expect to have questions about the text. Also know that exploring the Bible can be a daunting job for anyone. But be assured, too, that there are many excellent references to help a person. Here is an overview of the most common types of helps:

Reference materials, short versions of the materials described below, are often printed in the backs of some Bibles. The references are printed as separate volumes, however, and cover topics more extensively.

An **annotated or study Bible** typically contains introductions to the books of the Bible; brief outlines of the books; notes on difficult verses or words; chapter outlines; and articles of general interest on history and geography, translations, and Bible study methods.

The best commentary on the Bible is often a text from another part of the Bible. Therefore, it is often helpful to check the **cross-references**. A cross-reference lists a Bible verse followed by references to one or more related or similar verses. Study Bibles have the most important cross-references listed either in a center column or at the bottom of the page. Cross-references are also known as parallel passages.

A **concordance** helps you locate a Bible passage when you know only a word or phrase from the verse. There are separate concordances for each major translation of the Bible. Find one written for your Bible's translation. To use a concordance, look up a key word from the passage you want to find. Following the word is a list of verses, along with the portion of each passage that includes the key word.

For example, to find the verse that starts "God so loved the world…" look up the word *world*. Notice that the Bible verses are listed in the order they appear in the Bible. Scan the verses. After John 3:16 you will find the phrase, "God so loved the *w.*" You can look up the passage, explore the surrounding text, and check cross-references.

When you decide which word to look up, choose one that is important in the verse but that is not too common. In this case, for example, you would not look up *God* or *love* because there would be too many references to review easily.

A concordance also helps you do a word study. By checking many references that include the same word, you can explore the way that word is used in the Bible. Often a passage becomes clearer when a key word is understood in a new light.

A **commentary** includes the biblical text plus a verse-by-verse explanation of the Bible. A commentary provides more detail than a study Bible. There are one-volume commentaries on the entire Bible, as well as commentaries with separate volumes for individual books or the books of the Bible.

Handbooks of the Bible do not reprint the text of the Bible, but the articles, which can be extensive, follow the order of the Bible.

A Bible **dictionary** contains short articles on words and topics such as people named in the Bible, groups such as the Pharisees, geography and history, culture, animals, and rituals.

An **atlas** of the Bible, often included in other reference books, provides maps of the Bible lands at various periods of history. You might find helpful a map of Bible lands that prints both the current and ancient names of places.

From *Bible Reading Handbook* by Paul Schuessler, copyright © 1991 Augsburg Fortress.

Bible Bookmarks

**Luke 2:1-20
The Birth of Jesus**

Christmas Prayer

Almighty God, you have made yourself known in your Son, Jesus, redeemer of the world. We pray that his birth as a human child will set us free from the old slavery of our sin. Amen.

**Matthew 3:13-17
The Baptism of Jesus**

Baptism Prayer

Gracious God, at the baptism of Jesus you proclaimed him your beloved Son and anointed him with the Holy Spirit. Make all who are baptized into Christ faithful in their calling to be your children and inheritors with him of everlasting life. Amen.

**Luke 4:1-13
The Temptation of Jesus**

Prayer for Guidance

Direct us, O Lord, in all our doings with your most gracious favor and further us with your continual help, that in all our works, begun, continued, and ended in you, we may glorify your holy name. Amen.

**Mark 11:15-19
The Cleansing of the Temple**

Prayer for Perspective

O God, you have given us gifts which our forbearers neither knew nor dreamed of. Grant that we may not be so occupied with material things that we forget the things which are spiritual and thus, even though we have gained the whole world, lose our souls. Amen.

**Matthew 5:1-12
The Sermon on the Mount**

Prayer of Response to Blessings

O Lord our God, maker of all things. Through your goodness you have blessed us with many gifts. With them we offer ourselves to your service and dedicate our lives to the care and redemption of all that you have made. Amen.

**Mark 2:1-12
The Healing of the Paralytic**

Prayer for Healing

God of all mercy, by your power to heal and to forgive, graciously cleanse us from all sin and make us strong. Amen.

**Matthew 26:17-30
The Lord's Supper**

Prayer for After Holy Communion

Almighty God, you provide the true bread from heaven, your Son, Jesus Christ our Lord. Grant that we who have received the Sacrament of his body and blood may abide in him and he in us, that we may be filled with the power of his endless life, now and forever. Amen.

**Mark 15:21-39
The Crucifixion**

Prayer for Good Friday

Lord Jesus, you carried our sins in your own body on the tree so that we might have life. May we and all who remember this day find new life in you now and in the world to come. Amen.

**Luke 24:13-35
The Road to Emmaus**

Prayer for Travellers

Lord God, you kept Abraham and Sarah in safety during their pilgrimage, you led the children of Israel through the sea, and by a star you led the Wise Men to Jesus. Protect and guide us in our time of travel, make our ways safe and our homecomings joyful. Amen.

**Acts 1:6-11
The Ascension**

Prayer for the Ascension of Our Lord

Almighty God, your only Son was taken up into heaven and in power intercedes for us. May we also come into your presence and live forever in your glory. Amen.

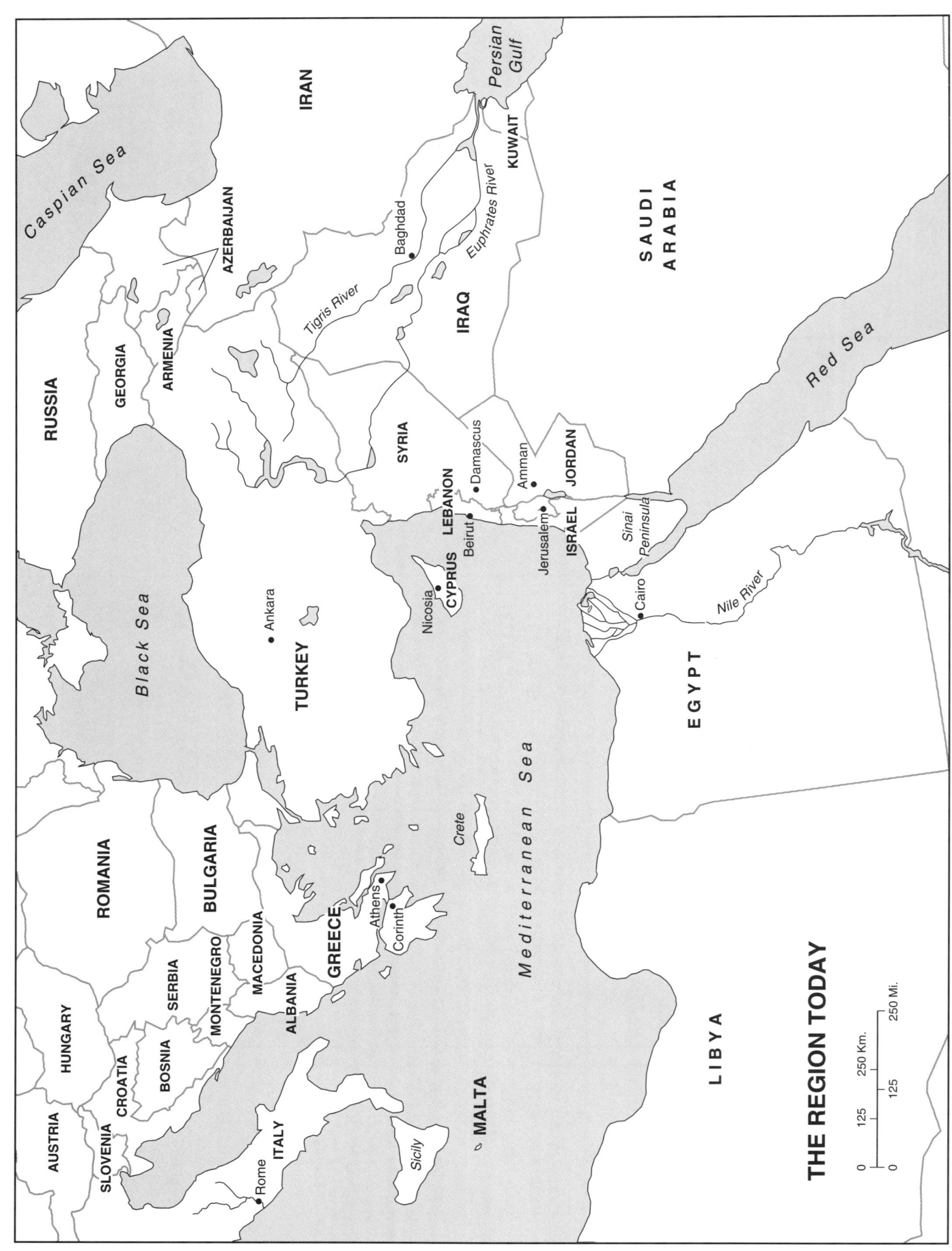

THE REGION TODAY

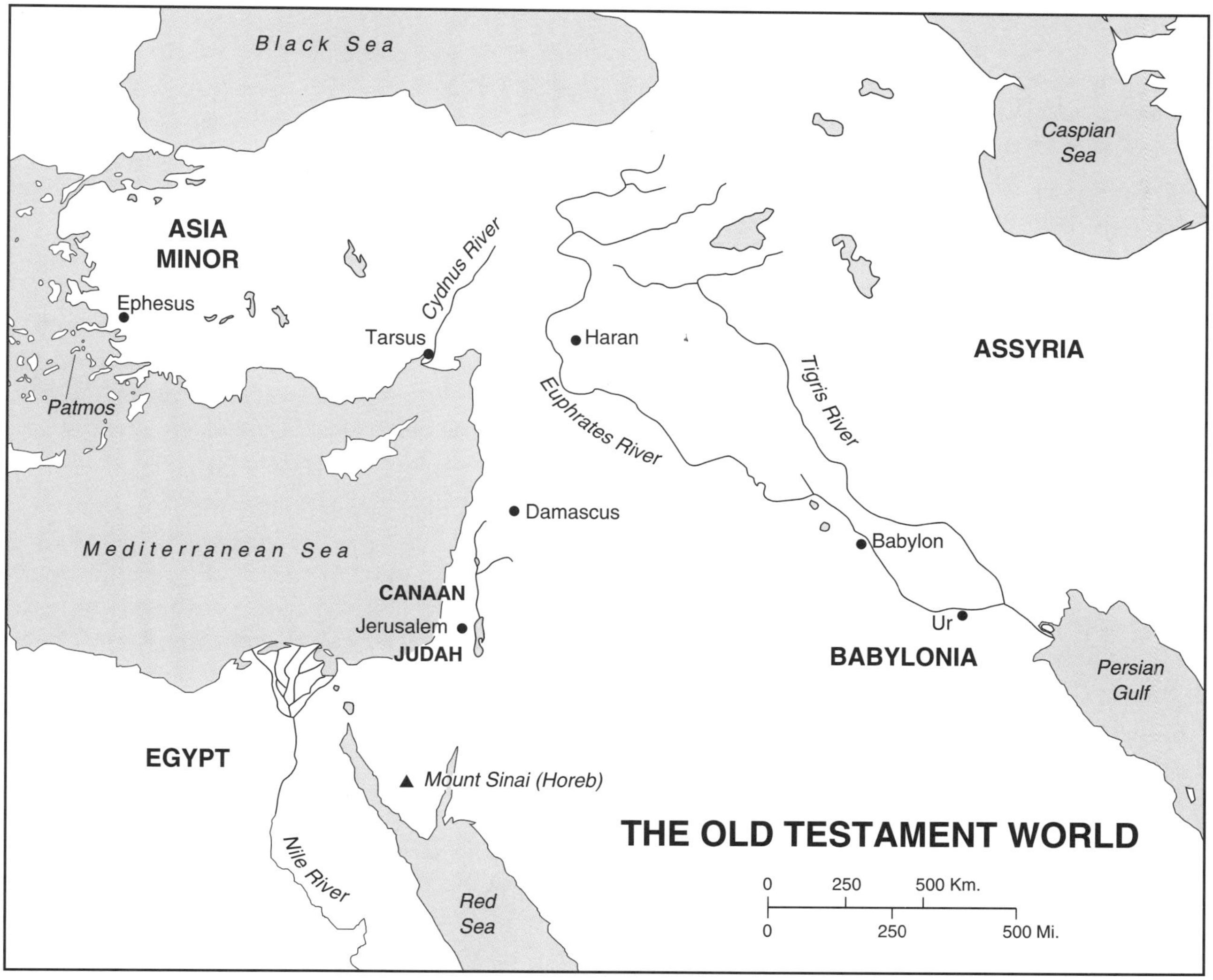

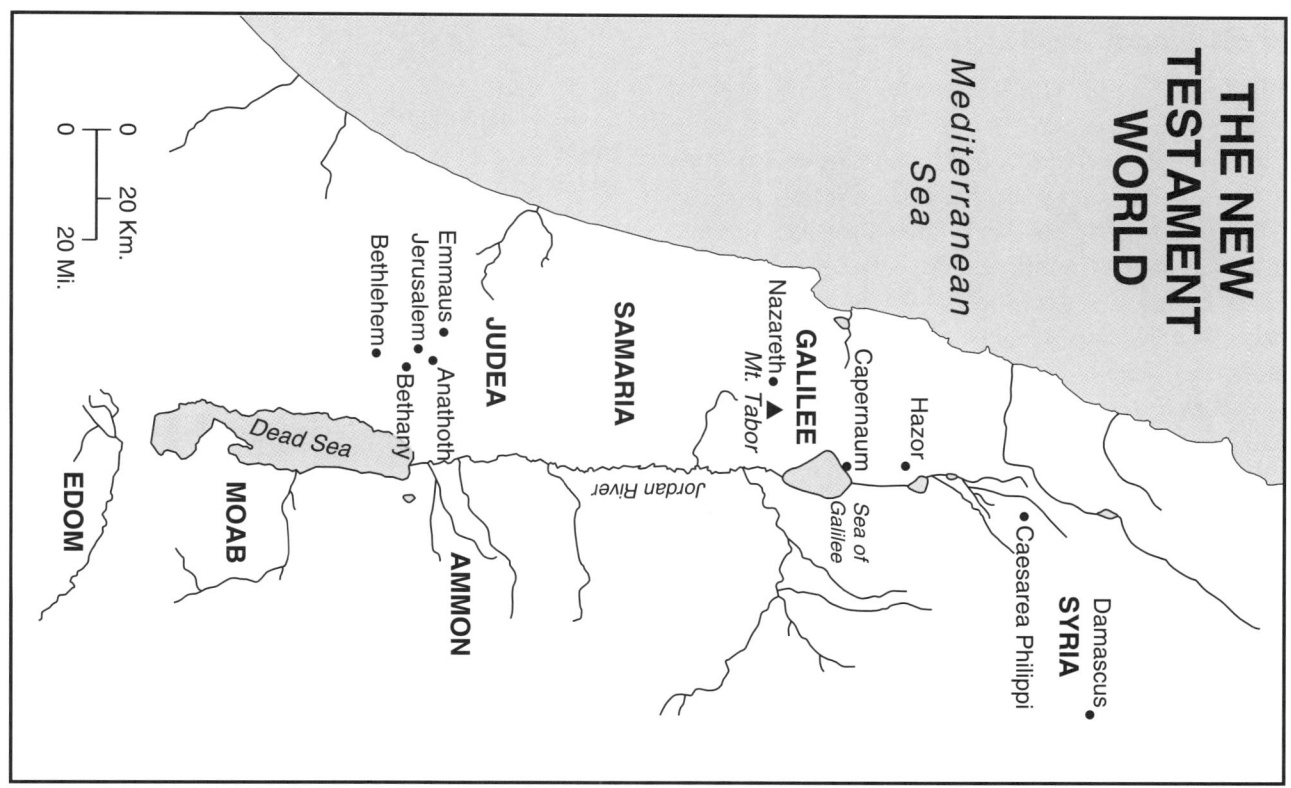

THE OLD TESTAMENT WORLD

Black Sea

Caspian Sea

ASIA MINOR

ASSYRIA

• Ephesus

Tarsus

Cydnus River

• Haran

Tigris River

Euphrates River

Patmos

Mediterranean Sea

• Damascus

• Babylon

CANAAN

Jerusalem •
JUDAH

Ur •

BABYLONIA

Persian Gulf

EGYPT

▲ *Mount Sinai (Horeb)*

0	250	500 Km.
0	250	500 Mi.

Nile River

Red Sea

THE NEW TESTAMENT WORLD

Mediterranean Sea

0	
0	
20 Km.	
20 Mi.	

Emmaus •
Jerusalem •
Bethlehem •

• Anathoth
• Bethany

JUDEA

SAMARIA

Nazareth •
▲ *Mt. Tabor*

GALILEE

Capernaum

Hazor •

Dead Sea

EDOM

MOAB

AMMON

Jordan River

Sea of Galilee

• Caesarea Philippi

Damascus •
SYRIA

The Bible in Worship

THE BIBLE IS AT THE CENTER of Christian worship. From the Bible comes much of the content and the general form of our worship. Each Sunday, for example, as many as three different "lessons" or "readings" are used.

In most mainline Christian congregations, the lessons follow a schedule of Bible readings, called the lectionary, that is repeated every three years. The lectionary, in turn, follows the church year, which begins by preparing us for the birth of Christ; continues with a focus on his suffering, death, and resurrection; and ends with an overview of Jesus' teachings.

All the readings reflect the theme for the Sunday's worship. The sermon, hymns, prayers, and other elements of the service further illuminate the central message.

The First Lesson is usually from the Old Testament, and the main point of the lesson is usually parallel to the main point of the Gospel lesson (see below). Often the congregation responds to this lesson by singing (or reading) a psalm, an ancient Hebrew hymn that was first used in worship in Old Testament times.

The Second Lesson is from one of the New Testament letters, the Book of Hebrews, or the Acts of the Apostles. Many of these writings were originally intended to be used in public worship.

The reading of **the Gospel** has always occupied a place of honor in worship. In most churches, the congregation stands during this reading in honor of Christ, whose life and words the Gospels relate.

The basic form of worship follows a pattern we can trace to the earliest Christians: "They devoted themselves to the apostles' teaching and fellowship, to the breaking of bread and the prayers" (Acts 2:42). We attend to the Word of God, and we share the Meal, Holy Communion.

The liturgy provides a pattern of spoken and sung texts that give flesh to the basic Word/Meal framework. Many parts of the liturgy are from Scripture. While denominations have a variety of traditions, these examples might be familiar to you:

The Greeting, "The grace of our Lord Jesus Christ, the love of God, and the communion of the Holy Spirit be with you all," is from 2 Corinthians 13:14. The verse is the closing of this letter from Paul to the church in Corinth.

The Hymn of Praise, which begins, "Glory to God in the highest," recalls the hymn the angels sang in the fields outside Bethlehem to announce Jesus' birth (Luke 2:14).

After **the offering** has been received, especially when Holy Communion is not celebrated, some congregations sing several verses from Psalm 51: "Create in me a clean heart, O God, and renew a right spirit within me…" (verses 10-12).

The liturgy for Holy Communion incorporates a number of Bible texts. **The Sanctus,** "Holy, holy, holy Lord, God of pow'r and might," sung near the beginning of this portion of the liturgy, is based on Isaiah 6:3. The prophet Isaiah was in the temple and saw a vision of angels, who sang this hymn of praise. (The word *sanctus* is Latin for "holy.")

The Words of Institution ("In the night in which he was betrayed, our Lord Jesus took bread…. Again, after supper, he took the cup….") do not have a single source. The narrative is a composition based on Matthew 26:26-28; Mark 14:22-25; Luke 22:17-20; and 1 Corinthians 11:23-26.

After Communion has been served, the congregation may join in the **hymn of thanks** that a devout, elderly man, Simeon, sang as he cradled the baby Jesus in his arms (Luke 2:29-32).

One customary **benediction,** or blessing, at the end of the service is from Numbers 6:24-27. God commanded Israel's leader, Aaron, to bless the people with words similar to these: "The Lord bless you and keep you. The Lord make his face shine on you and be gracious to you. The Lord look upon you with favor and give you peace."

Some congregations use another benediction, "Almighty God, Father, Son, and Holy Spirit, bless you now and forever." This blessing recalls Jesus' last words to his disciples before he ascended into heaven (Matthew 28:19).

Using These Resources in Other Settings

TODAY'S NORM for scheduling Christian education opportunities involves flexibility and choices. **Bible Basics for Adults** resources have been designed with this in mind. Each course has been designed for use in six sessions that may vary in length from 45 to 60 minutes. Although this structure will work for many adults, the reality is that today's learners have diverse and unpredictable schedules. Therefore, different options must be available to complete a study.

We learn the biblical message and its importance for our lives in a variety of settings. Corporate worship, devotions, class discussions, retreats, and personal conversations represent some of the ways we learn about the Bible. It is therefore valuable to be open to different possibilities that can help adults begin the journey of studying the Bible as part of their Christian life and faith.

Encourage people to participate in the course by providing alternatives to help learners who cannot attend six weekly sessions.

Mentoring

A study group may want to encourage participants to serve as mentors to one another when someone is absent for a particular session. For example, if Sally is unable to attend a session, Juanita, a fellow learner in the class, could meet with or telephone Sally and share some of the key discussions and learning that Juanita recalls from the time the group last met. This way Sally remains connected to the course material, and Juanita enjoys the pleasure of serving a neighbor and reinforcing her own learning at the same time. This experience not only helps Sally and Juanita review biblical material, it also helps Sally remember she is a valued member of the group.

Retreats

Entirely different educational environments can also be explored. A one-day event or an overnight retreat can provide meaningful alternatives to a weekly class schedule. In either case, the course material can be woven together with worship, community building activities, small group work, games, singing, reflection exercises, and more. All of these possibilities can be developed from recommendations in the leader guide and learner book.

Independent Study

Recognizing that not all adults are willing to study in groups nor able to fit into specific class schedules, another educational format could be an independent study that involves a mentor who helps guide the learning process. This way it is easier to find times when people can meet, discuss the sessions, and learn together. A slight variation of this approach would be to give an individual both the leader guide and learner book and allow that person to study independently. It would still be good in this scenario to have two or three meetings with another person to reflect upon the insights, questions, concerns, and commitments that emerge from studying the Bible.

Lifelong Learning

Whatever options are explored to help adults begin the journey of lifelong study of the Bible, a primary goal is to learn about the Bible in the context of a community's nurturing relationships. This reflects the important principle that building and maintaining caring relationships is integral to Christian education. It reminds us that the Holy Spirit works in our lives through others (1 Corinthians 12:7). The benefit of this goal and principle is the experience of growing in faith through the service, insights, support, and modeling of others.

Glossary

Blasphemy. The crime of which Jesus was accused (Mark 14:61-64). It is saying and doing things contrary to the will of God and/or claiming the authority reserved for God. (Session 4)

Centurion. A Roman army officer in charge of 100 men. (Session 4)

Disciple. This word means "student," one who was a follower of Jesus. (Sessions 2, 5)

Emmanuel. A name for Jesus meaning "God is with us." (Session 1)

Gospel. The word means "good news." It is the title given to each of the first four books of the New Testament. (Sessions 1, 3, 4, 5)

Grace. God's love to all. This love is not deserved or earned by the recipients. (Session 3)

Joshua. The Hebrew name for *Jesus* meaning "savior." (Session 1)

Messiah. A Hebrew title given Jesus that means "the Anointed One." The Greek word for *Messiah* is "Christ." (Session 5)

Passover. The event that remembered the Angel of Death passing over the children of Israel while they were slaves in Israel (Exodus 12:1-28). (Session 4)

Rabbi. The title given to the religious clergy of Israel. The word means "teacher." (Sessions 2, 3, 5)

Repent. To turn around and change one's way of life. (Session 1)

Sanhedrin. The Jewish religious court that brought Jesus to trial. (Session 4)

Shema. The ancient creed of Israel from Deuteronomy 6:4 "Hear O Israel, the Lord is One." (Session 1)

Son of God. A title given to Jesus by the centurion who was a witness to Jesus' crucifixion. (Session 4)

Son of man. A title given to Jesus especially in the Gospel of Mark (Mark 2:10; 9:9; 14:62; and others). (Session 3)

Synagogue. A local religious place of worship in Jesus' day. (Session 3)

Theophilus. The man to whom Luke addressed both the Gospel of Luke and the Book of Acts. It means "lover of God" (Luke 1:3, Acts 1:1). (Sessions 4, 5)